Feminine Callings

Celebrating the 10th Anniversary of the
2011 Goddess Summit
and The Goddess Show series!

Matrika Press

"Twinkle" Marie Manning

Feminine Callings
Celebrating the 10th Anniversary of the
2011 Goddess Summit and The Goddess Show series!

Copyright © "Twinkle" Marie Porter-Manning
October 2021

All Rights Reserved
including the right of reproduction,
copying, or storage in any form
or means, including electronic,
In Whole or Part,
without prior written
permission of the author.

ISBN: 978-1-946088-64-2
Library of Congress Control Number: 2021948819

1.Goddess Culture 2.Sacred-Feminine 3.Self-Exploration
4.Religion 5.Divinity 6.Spirituality 7.Philosophy
8.Keepsake 9.Title

Matrika Press

Matrika Press
P.O. Box 115
Rockwood, Maine 04478
Editor@MatrikaPress.com

www.MatrikaPress.com

*Please note, images contained in this book are of the highest quality we could produce from screenshots with current technology available.

Table of Contents

Prologue
4

ALisa Starkweather
6

Dale Allen
10

Elinor Gadon
14

Isadora Leidenfrost
18

Kiana Love
22

Lisa Campion
26

Margaret Stewart
30

Serpentessa
34

Starhawk
38

Elizabeth Stahl
42

Lara Berry
46

"Twinkle" Marie Manning
50

Additional Photo Gallery Images
54

Other Works by "Twinkle" Marie Manning
58

About Matrika Press
64

Prologue

Autumn 2021 marks the ten year anniversary of the the *2011 Goddess Summit* hosted by "Twinkle" Marie Manning. This event was followed by one-on-one interviews in our studios for *The Goddess Show* series. Such was the beginning of a multi-year journey of recording sessions, in-studio and on-location, capturing interviews rooted in exploring the Sacred Feminine & Great Mysteries. In total, nine guests were interviewed by three hosts.

Featured guests include:
ALisa Starkweather, Dale Allen, Elinor Gadon, Isadora Leidenfrost, Kiana Love, Lisa Campion, Margaret Stewart, Serpentessa, and *Starhawk.* Hosts leading these interviews are: *Elizabeth Stahl, Lara Berry* and *"Twinkle" Marie Manning.*

Though several attempts were made over the years to complete the project by a diverse selection of editors and production assistants, it seemed much of the original footage was unusable for various reasons, including cameras running hot and intricate audio issues.

Summer 2021 found "Twinkle" Marie Manning, executive producer of the project, taking yet another glance through the footage as part of a completion ritual as she prepares for the next phase of her life. She found that she was finally able to extract usable portions. With excitement, awe, relief and delight she began to weave together what she could.

The content from the show and the summit have been transformed into brief excerpts, full-length interviews, a documentary, and other media with the express goal of sharing these vital messages with the world.

This media archive is made possible via *TV for Your Soul*, *Empowering Women TV* and *Matrika Press*.

Most of the one-on-one interviews were recorded at *LexMedia*, in Lexington, Massachusetts. We are thankful to the staff and team of volunteers who helped with this project. We are grateful to *Jeannette Kearny* for opening her beautiful home to make space to hold the *2011 Goddess Summit*.

It is with gratitude we dedicate this book to the women featured on video: our guests and our hosts. Your feminine callings bring meaning to many. You are inspirations, indeed, beacons lighting the paths of past, present and future.

May it ever be so.

ALisa Starkweather

ALisa Starkweather is the founder of many powerful women's initiatives, including: the Red Tent Temple Movement, Daughters of the Earth Gatherings, the Women's Belly and Womb Conferences, the women's mystery school, Priestess Path Apprenticeship and co-founder of the international women's initiation, Women in Power; Initiating Ourselves to the Predator Within. She is a Shadow Work and breathwork facilitator as well as a keynote speaker and life coach.

Thirty-five years of dedication to women's empowerment gave her a reputation where she is known for her passionate archetypal work that focuses on transformation, healing, community, ritual and the rebalancing of the sacred feminine.

ALisa was interviewed on the set of *The Goddess Show* by Elizabeth Stahl. During the interview she shared her gifts of singing, chanting and drumming. She was also one of the predominantly featured feminine spiritual leaders in the *2011 Goddess Summit*. Throughout her years of dedicated work, she has helped generations of women discover their voices, cherish their bodies and claim their authentic paths.

> www.TVforYourSoul.org/alisa-starkweather
> https://new.alisastarkweather.com
> http://redtenttemplemovement.com

8.

Pictures spread of ALisa Starkweather on *The Goddess Show* set with, Elizabeth Stahl, Lara Berry, "Twinkle" Marie Manning, and Twinkle's son Orion along with Serpentessa's snakes.

Dale Allen

Dale Allen is a veteran of corporate, commercial communications. Her extensive resume includes hundreds of voice-over, on-camera and live presentation project. Her energy and enthusiasm, sincerity and strength infuse her presentations and impact audiences. Dale was honored to twice present to the United Nations Commission on the Status of Women, her one-woman show, In Our Right Minds™, Guiding Women to Their Strength as Leaders, Leading Men to Strength Without Armor.

She has brought her talents to scores of audiences – nationwide, to Canada, and from Kauai to Dubai. Described as having the energy of "a Cape Canaveral liftoff," she thoroughly engages and inspires her audience, which ranges from highly educated corporate leaders to teenage girls seeking their place in the world.

Dale was one of our most dynamic participants in the *2011 Goddess Summit*, and as one of our featured guests in *The Goddess Show* where she was interviewed by Elizabeth Stahl. Dale's powerful magnetism comes through the screen. We are blessed to share her enthusiasm for accessing the divine feminine and women's empowerment.

www.TVforYourSoul.org/dale-allen

https://DaleAllenProductions.com

Pictures spread of Dale Allen on *The Goddess Show* and *Goddess Summit* sets with, Elizabeth Stahl and "Twinkle" Marie Manning..

Elinor Gadon

We are ever so grateful to have captured two interviews with the iconic scholar Elinor Gadon. Both Elizabeth Stahl and "Twinkle" Marie Manning had one-on-one conversations with Elinor during her time in our studios.

Elinor Gadon is an American cultural historian and art historian specializing in Indian art and culture. Her work delves deep into the analysis of images and symbols in their cultural context. She known for her examination of women in myth and culture in history. She has taught at Harvard, Tufts, and the New School for Social Research. Elinor is the author of the iconic book entitled, *The Once and Future Goddess: A Sweeping Visual Chronicle of the Sacred Female and Her Reemergence in the Cultural Mythology of our Time*. Her work has influenced generations of people seeking accurate information about the feminine aspects of the divine and how such sacred symbolism has played a role throughout history. Among her many achievements, she was the recipient of the Honor Award for Lifetime Achievement in the Visual Arts from the Women's Caucus for Art, and of the Demeter Award for Leadership in Women's Spirituality from the Association for the Study of Women and Mythology in 2016. To our program she brought erudite acumen.

Elinor transitioned from life on Earth on May 8th, 2018. It is with fondness and gratitude we remember Elinor.

www.TVforYourSoul.org/elinor-gadon

Pictures spread of Elinor Gadon on *The Goddess Show* set with Elizabeth Stahl and "Twinkle" Marie Manning.

Isadora Leidenfrost

Dr. Isadora Leidenfrost is an award-winning filmmaker and highly sought after creative talent. Her work has been seen on PBS, Amazon Prime, and thousands of independent screenings worldwide. She is a multi-talented filmmaker, designer, photographer, public speaker, author, and all-around creative businesswoman and visionary entrepreneur.

She holds a PhD and a Masters from the University of Wisconsin-Madison and a BFA from the Rhode Island School of Design (RISD). Isadora has a sweet, generous spirit that fosters collaborations among peers.

During her interview with Elizabeth Stahl for *The Goddess Show* series, she speaks robustly about her groundbreaking 72-minute documentary entitled: *Things We Don't Talk About: Woman's Stories from the Red Tent*. She also shares her journey as a citizen of the world, a woman on the goddess path, and a filmmaker focused on female empowerment.

Isadora's message is one of courage and liberation.

www.TVforYourSoul.com/isadora-leidenfrost
www.soulfulmedia.com/about-dr-isadora
www.redtentmovie.com

20.

Pictures spread of Isadora Leidenfrost on *The Goddess Show* set with Elizabeth Stahl and "Twinkle" Marie Manning. Also pictured is her legendary "Red Tent" sculpture, created by artist Teresa Moorehouse in support of Isadora's film project.

Kiana Love

22.

Kiana Love is the founder of Be Wild Woman.

She is an energy healer who helps overwhelmed women and survivors of childhood trauma feel safe and loved, so they can trust themselves, find freedom in their bodies, and enjoy their lives.

Yes, Kiana's teachings and work lead women to the understanding that when a woman begins to trust herself, she learns the answers to questions she is seeking are already inside of her. As a result, they begin to have more peace of mind and freedom to be themselves. They are empowered to feel confident, creative, curious, are filled with courage to speak their truth, ask for what they want—and get it— each and every day!

Kiana holds a B.S. in Behavioral Science from the University of Houston, and has certifications in somatic healing and holistic health. She is a Wild Woman Healer, Reiki Master, Integrated Energy Therapy Instructor, Vortex Healer, Intuitive, Holistic Health Counselor, Herbalist, Reflexologist, Interfaith Minister and Yoga Teacher.

Kiana was a pivotal member of the 2011 *Goddess Summit*. Her keen intuition, passionate telling of her personal story, and leadership as she guides women towards discovering their own sacred-selves generates immense healing. Kiana was interviewed afterwards at our studio by Lara Berry for *The Goddess Show* series.

www.TVforYourSoul.com/kiana-love

www.bewildwoman.com

24.

Pictures spread of Kiana Love on *The Goddess Show* and *Goddess Summit* sets with Margaret Stewart, Dale Allen and "Twinkle" Marie Manning.

Lisa Campion

Lisa Campion has been a practicing psychic for decades. She uses a combination of intuition, energy healing and therapeutic techniques to help clients understand themselves at a deeper soul level.

She is the Dean of Students at Rhys Thomas Institute of Energy Medicine as well as one of their lead teachers. The three-year program she teaches trains healers in: Full Spectrum healing techniques, advanced energy anatomy, psychological and spiritual assessment and diagnostic tools.

Lisa's specialty as a psychic counselor is to work at the level of the soul, and she works with people at all levels of crossroads and transitions, be they amid a crisis or simply seeking guidance on their paths.

In 2011 our hosts and crew went on-location to Lisa Campion's studio! The framing of her interview is distinct from the conversations we hosted in-studio in both setting and style. Throughout Lisa demonstrates her empathic abilities to connect with viewers while offering a unique lens to paths that lead to the Goddess.

Special thanks to Martha Kilcoyne for leading the interview off-camera.

www.TVforYourSoul.com/lisa-campion
https://lisacampion.com

28.

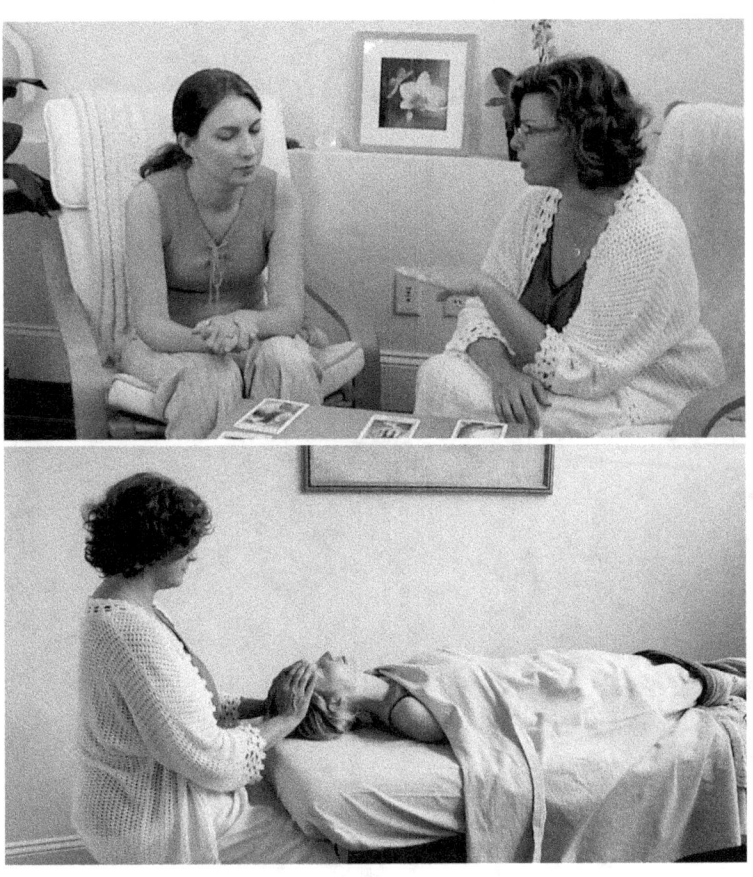

Pictures spread of Lisa Campion being recorded for *The Goddess Show* series with Lara Berry and "Twinkle" Marie Manning.
Additionally pictured is a beautiful triple-goddess ornament in her studio.

Margaret Stewart

Margaret Stewart is a matriarch in the sacred feminine Goddess tradition where she was the founder and leader of the Concord, Massachusetts-based Women's Goddess Covenant Circle for many years.

Margaret's presence and voice at the table of the 2011 *Goddess Summit* set a solid foundation in the conversation from which we could build upon.

Drawing on her wisdom of the ancient, made relevant to the new, revealed her as one of the authentic foremothers of our modern-day Goddess Culture.

Margaret brought with her a sacred artifact dating back many millennia. The carved stone artifact, when held by each woman present, resonated its ancestral purpose in unspoken prose.

In addition to participating in the Summit, she was interviewed by Lara Berry as part of *The Goddess Show* series where she shared more details of her journey with the Goddess and within the ranks of 2nd Wave Feminism. Margaret discussed the distinction of being in the lap of the Goddess, and various aspects of the divine feminine archetypes (Maiden, Mother, Crone) to which she is drawn to. She also described the kinds of spiritual practices and rituals she has participated in and led over the years within her circle of women. Margaret now resides in Arizona.

www.TVforYourSoul.com/margaret-stewart

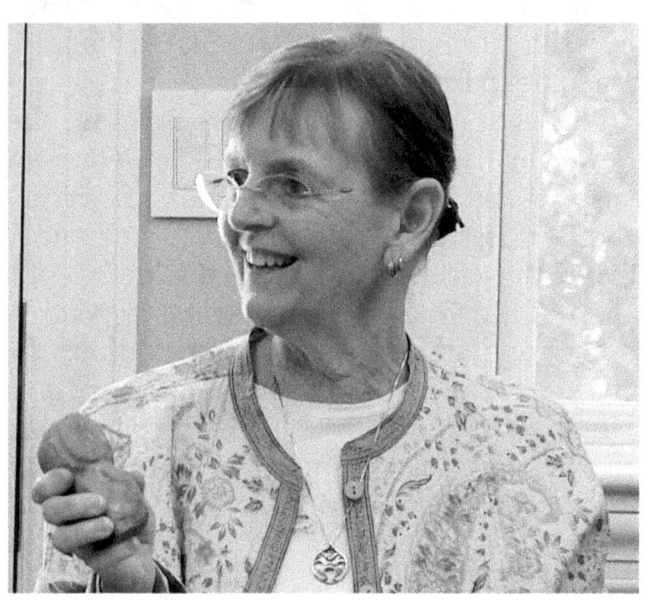

Pictures spread of Margaret Stewart on the sets of the 2011 *Goddess Summit* and *The Goddess Show* series with Lara Berry, ALisa Starkweather, Kiana Love and "Twinkle" Marie Manning.
Additionally pictured is the ancient 10,000 year old goddess artifact Margaret brought with her to share during the Goddess Summit.

Serpentessa

Serpentessa is a modern day Snake Priestess who practices Ancient Snake Medicine. Along with her Snakes as teachers, she works with individuals and groups who desire to be in the Garden of Earth. She is said to skillfully facilitate emotional journeys with her Snakes in a hands-on encounter to create the results wanted in one's life. Her services are valued by spirit-led, wise-women leaders, nature lovers and heartfelt coaches desiring transformative Snake Encounters of Presence, Pleasure, Power and Purpose.

Serpentessa joined our gathering at the *2011 Goddess Summit*, as well was interviewed by Elizabeth Stahl in our Lexington, MA studio for an episode of *The Goddess Show* series. As part of the recording session, she guided Elizabeth through a Snake Journey ritual.

Those present at the studio during the recording session, including Lara Berry, ALisa Starkweather, "Twinkle" Marie Manning, and her young son, Orion, were also able to get up close and personal with Serpentessa's snake friends.

∞ Belly to belly, skin to skin,
we and snakes and earth are kin. ∞

www.TVforYourSoul.com/serpentessa
http://serpentessa.com

Pictures spread of Serpentessa on the set of the *The Goddess Show* series with her snake friends, as well as Elizabeth Stahl, Lara Berry, ALisa Starkweather, "Twinkle" Marie Manning, and Twinkle's son Orion.

Starhawk

Starhawk is one of the prominent leaders in the revival of earth-based spirituality and Goddess religion. She is a co-founder of Reclaiming, an activist branch of modern Pagan religion, and continues to work closely with the Reclaiming Community. Her archives are maintained at the Graduate Theological Union library in Berkeley, CA. She is an activist, permaculture designer and teacher, and a prominent voice in modern earth-based spirituality and ecofeminism.

Starhawk is an award winning author and co-author of many books, including *The Spiral Dance: A Rebirth of the Ancient Religion of the Great Goddess; The Empowerment Manual: A Guide for Collaborative Groups; Dreaming the Dark: Magic, Sex, and Politics; Circle Round: Raising Children in the Goddess Tradition;* the ecotopian novel *The Fifth Sacred Thing* and its sequel, *City of Refuge;* and a picture book for children entitled, *The Last Wild Witch.*

Starhawk founded Earth Activist Training, teaching permaculture design grounded in spirituality and with a focus on activism. She travels internationally, lecturing and teaching on earth-based spirituality, the tools of ritual, and the skills of activism.

In June 2014 Starhawk was interviewed in our Lexington, MA studios by "Twinkle" Marie Manning.

Starhawk and Twinkle also co-led a women's spiritual gathering in Concord, MA.

www.TVforYourSoul.com/starhawk
https://starhawk.org

Minerva Potluck followed by Starhawk's Women's Workshop + Spiral Dance: June 3rd, 2014

- Creating Sacred Community
- Holding Our Own Power
- Stepping into Leadership.

Followed by <u>Spiral Dance</u> on the Labyrinth

Hosted by
"Twinkle" Marie Manning

Tickets available online: www.TVforYourSoul.com/STARHAWK.html

Pictures spread of Starhawk on the set of the *The Goddess Show* series with cast, crew and some audience members. As well, pictures of Starhawk during her stay with "Twinkle" Marie Manning in Concord, Massachusetts. Including a women's empowerment workshop, luncheons and breakfasts with friends, plus a visit to Walden Pond with Twinkle, Karen Kashian, and Twinkle's son Orion. Some of those pictured include: Cynthia Ellis, Lois Suarez, Lara Berry, Erin Diskin, Lana Bastianutti Margaret Stewart, Bozena & Irl Smith, Suzanne Foley, Lois Whitney, and Polly Peterson.

Elizabeth Stahl

Elizabeth Stahl is a Women and Girls Empowerment Facilitator; Public Speaker; Priestess and self-proclaimed Goddess. She is passionate about the health and well-being of girls and women everywhere. She is the creator of classes, workshops and celebratory gatherings known as the *Goddess Party, WomanMind, Girls of Power, Soaring Beauty* and the *Goddessy Odyssey*. She hosts these gatherings for women of all ages during times of transition and celebration. Such gatherings take the shape of Bridal Showers, Bachelorette Parties, Baby Showers, Blessing Ways, Bat-Mitzvah's, and even Girls Nights Out!

Elizabeth is the co-Author of two powerful coaching books: *In Her Power – A Woman's Guide to Purpose, Peace and Play* and *Top Coaches Share – Their Personal Power Strategies.*

Elizabeth Stahl came to our **TV for Your Soul** family as part of a large group that was curated during the 2009-2013 period where in collaboration with local television studios volunteers created more than 10 new programs! Elizabeth was one of three hosts for *The Goddess Show*! During her time with *TV for Your Soul*, Elizabeth interviewed ALisa Starkweather, Dale Allen, Isadora Leidenfrost and Elinor Gadon. Elizabeth also participated in the *2011 Goddess Summit*. We are grateful for her leadership and enthusiasm.

www.TVforYourSoul.org/elizabeth-stahl
https://www.elizabeth-stahl.com/goddess-parties.html

44.

Pictures spread of Elzabeth Stahl on the sets of the 2011 *Goddess Summit* and *The Goddess Show* series with "Twinkle" Marie Manning, Lara Berry, Dale Allen, Elinor Gadon, ALisa Starkweather, and Serpentessa.

Lara Berry

Lara Berry is an esteemed Library Director, TV talk show host, author and publisher. She co-hosted *Two Scrybes* television series, produced at PPMtv studios in New Hampshire, which featured interviews with local guest authors. Lara received a Master of Education at Plymouth State University.

At the 2011 *Goddess Summit* Lara was one of the lead guides, as well as a host for *The Goddess Show* series. During the one-on-one conversation segments, she interviewed Margaret Stewart and Kiana Love.

Lara joined our **TV for Your Soul** family during a busy period when we were bustling in the creation of several new programs. She brought with her a light and insight that helped shaped the focus and illuminate the spectrum of our sacred-feminine, Goddess-dedicated programs.

Lara's personal dedication to the Goddess is inspirational to many, as are her commitment to justice and healing. Her thoughtful interview style created sacred space for guests to share deeply with her, and with our viewers.

www.TVforYourSoul.org/lara-berry

Pictures spread of Lara Berry on the sets of the 2011 *Goddess Summit* and *The Goddess Show* series with "Twinkle" Marie Manning, Margaret Stewart, Kiana Love, ALisa Starkweather, and Serpentessa.

49.

"Twinkle" Marie Manning

Known as "Twinkle" by many, Marie Manning has been creating, producing and directing transformational media content for more than two decades. She is the founder and executive producer of *TV for Your Soul*. Her complete media resume is lengthy, as she has helped develop and support myriad projects for others in addition to her own, spanning such venues as live events, studio productions for both television and radio, as well as magazine and book publishing, often combining multimedia platforms for retreats and expo-style, fundraising events, conferences, concerts and salon gatherings.

Such collaborative projects with **TV for Your Soul** have included: *The Goddess Show; Goddess Summits, Body, Mind and Spirit; Room of One's Own, Contributions to Earth; Wedding Essentials, TEDxWaldenPond; Conversations* on PBS; *Celebrity Charities;* coverage of the *International Women's Day* and *One Billion Rising* Events and, of course, her *Empowering Women TV Series and Signature Events*. Twinkle has a unique ability to weave the secular with the spiritual in all platforms of her media ministry.

She interviewed Starhawk and Elinor Gadon and was the host of the *2011 Goddess Summit*.

"Twinkle" now resides in Maine where she is the lead minister of *The Church of Kineo* and founding facilitator for *Moosehead Lake Retreats*. She is an author, poet, artist, gatherer and grandmother.

www.TVforYourSoul.com/twinkle
www.TwinklesPlace.org

Pictures spread of "Twinkle" Marie Manning on the sets of the 2011 *Goddess Summit* and *The Goddess Show* series with Lara Berry, Elizabeth Stahl, Margaret Stewart, Kiana Love, ALisa Starkweather, Serpentessa, Dale Allen, Elinor Gadon and Starhawk. As well as images of Twinkle recording, directing and producing programs.

Additional Photo Gallery Images of the 2011 Goddess Summit & The Goddess Show Series

Starhawk's Chant:

What is on life
What it can do will fall
the power in your hand
to change it all

If you want to know
where the power lies
Turn and look into your
sister's eyes.

(D)
Turn and look into love
Other's eyes

Other Works by "Twinkle" Marie Manning

Women of Spirit, Exploring Sacred Paths of Wisdom Keepers is a compilation of women sojourners, sages, mystics, witches, shaman, medicine women, ministers, philosophers, therapists, life coaches, yogis, and more.

Their journeys.

Their stories.

Their teachings and practices.

Essays, Poetry, Art, Rituals and Prayers.

This anthology is full of useful tools and powerful messages for everyone who is on a spiritual journey to embrace and enjoy. Beloved Contributors include:

- *Anna Huckabee Tull*
- *Bernadette Rombough*
- *Deb Elbaum* • *Deborah Diamond*
- *Debra Wilson Guttas* • *Grace Ventura*
- *Janeen Barnett* • *JoAnne Bassett* • *Judy Ann Foster* • *Julie Matheson* • *Kate Early*
- *Kate Kavanagh* • *Katherine Glass* • *Kris Oster* • *Lea M. Hill* • *Meghan Gilroy*
- *Morwen Two Feathers* • *Rustie MacDonald* • *Shamanaca* • *Sharon Hinckley*
- *Shawna Allard* • *Shiloh Sophia* • *Susan Feathers* • *Tiffany Cano* • *Tory Londergan*
- *"Twinkle" Marie Porter-Manning* • *Tziporah Kingsbury* • *Valerie Sorrentino*

www.MatrikaPress.com/ twinkle-marie-manning

BLESSING BOOK SERIES

Uniquely designed to be journals, spiritual exploration tools and self-led retreats, *Blessing Books* can be used to mark a milestone such as a significant birthday or important season of your life. *Blessing Books* can help you process a loss or transition. It can be where you express your gratitude or your grief, and where you affirm what's present and next in your life. Wherever you are on your journey, and in both times of joy and in times of sorrow, may these books serve you well.

Divinely inspired. Practically written. *Living Life as a Prayer* presents a transformational theology that is accessible to everyone who wishes to embrace life in gratitude and grace. As a spiritual guidebook, *Living Life as a Prayer* outlines principles and practices to help us more deeply connect with that which we personally and uniquely identify as holy.

In her seminal work, Rev. Porter-Manning shepherds readers toward realizing our intrinsic connection to each other, and to the Divine.

Feminine Callings
By "Twinkle" Marie Manning

Tapestries of moments
Interwoven lives
Journeys of mutual acceptance
Guided by that which we call
Goddess
Nurtured by Nature
Emboldened by Essence
Culling fears
Healing through love
Traversing the unknown
Meeting at crossroads
Blessing thresholds
The wonder
The wandering
The shedding
The rooting
The soaring
Listening and answering
Individual callings
In awe of the mysteries
Embracing the sacred
Our bodies sublime
Our voices strong
Our spirits join
The feminine divine.

www.TwinklesPlace.org
www.MooseheadLakeRetreats.org
#LivingLifeAsAPrayer
#PiecesOfPeaceOnEarth

Matrika Press is an independent publishing house dedicated to publishing works in alignment with transformational religious and spiritual values and principles. Matrika Press has published anthologies, memoirs, poetry, prayer and ritual manuscripts, and other books to bring meaning and transformation to the world.

A primary goal of Matrika Press is to publish stories and works that would otherwise remain untold. We also resurrect out-of-print manuscripts to ensure our historical works remain accessible and publish transformational fiction for a small number of authors.

For information about how to collaborate on an anthology as a method of outreach and fundraising for your organization, congregation, business or group, email:
Editor@MatrikaPress.com

Why the name "Matrika"?
It is said that Matrika is the intrinsic energy or sound vibration of the 50 letters of the Sanskrit alphabet called *"The Mothers of Creation."* The Goddess Kali Ma used the letters to form words, and from the words formed all things. This aligns with scriptures that assert *"in the beginning was the Word,"* and in other sacred texts that affirm people of all backgrounds and faiths agree: *Words are powerful.* More than that: *Their vibrations are creative forces; they bring all things into being.*

www.ingramcontent.com/pod-product-compliance
Lightning Source LLC
Chambersburg PA
CBHW052123110526
44592CB00013B/1722